General George C. Marshall

World Leader

George Marshall was born on December 31, 1880 in Uniontown, Pennsylvania. He had an older brother named Stuart and a sister named Marie. George's father manufactured coking coal for the iron and steel industry.

Unscramble the sentence below to learn about George's family.

George was a distant relative of U.S. _____ Court _____
       MERESUP   JUCIEST

John _____.
      ALLMARSH

Coking coal is a special kind of coal good for melting iron ore. It burns very hot without creating smoke!

George attended school in Uniontown. George enjoyed playing football. He struggled with schoolwork, but did well in one subject.

Solve the code to discover something about George's favorite subject in school.

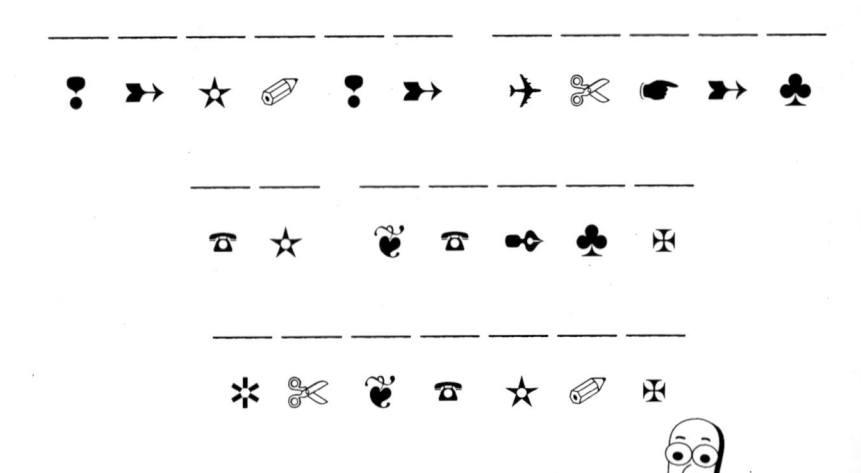

A	B	C	D	E	F	G	H	I	J	K	L	M
N	O	P	Q	R	S	T	U	V	W	X	Y	Z

___ ___ ___ ___ ___ ___ ___ ___ ___ ___ ___
F C B D F C L S J C D

___ ___ ___ ___ ___ ___ ___
T O R T U D Z

___ ___ ___ ___ ___ ___ ___ ___
G S R T O T P D Z

From an early age, George thought he wanted to be in the Army.

Page 2

When George was nine years old, his older brother, Stuart, enrolled at the Virginia Military Institute. Later, George begged his parents to send him, too. But, they did not have enough money.

Pull apart the sentence to find out how his family came up with the money to send George to the VMI.

Virginia Military Institute is also called the "VMI" for short.

His mother sold some property she owned in Kentucky.

One of George's distant cousins was Colonel Charles Marshall, who had been Robert E. Lee's aide during the Civil War.

George was accepted into the Virginia Military Institute. He was scheduled to start September 1, 1897, but during the summer he became very sick. He was still weak when he left for school.

Which "fever" did George suffer from in the summer of 1897?

The Virginia Military Institute is in Lexington, Virginia.

A. Hay fever

B. Typhoid fever

C. Disco fever

Typhoid fever is caused by bacteria. The bacteria make people weak, cause a fever, and sometimes people die!

George could not make it to the first day of school at the VMI. He was still sick from the fever. In fact, he didn't arrive until September 11, 1897.

First year students at the VMI are called "rats."

How many days late was George for the first day of school?

September 11 — Day George arrived
− September 1 — Day George should have arrived
_____

Number of days late

George's major at the VMI was Civil Engineering.

In 1901, George graduated with the rank of first captain of the Corps of Cadets. This was the highest rank in his class! In 1902, George was

Find the words in the Word Find below.

ARMY   MILITARY   RAT

During his first year at the VMI, a new central heating system and inside toilets were installed in the barracks!

George met Elizabeth "Lily" Carter Cole. He often left campus without permission to see her. In 1902, they were married.

P	L	C
A	I	N
K	T	A
S	O	L
M	R	L
A	G	A
Q	R	D
Y	R	Y

commissioned a second lieutenant in the Army. The U.S. Army was not as big then as it is today. George was not sure he would be accepted.

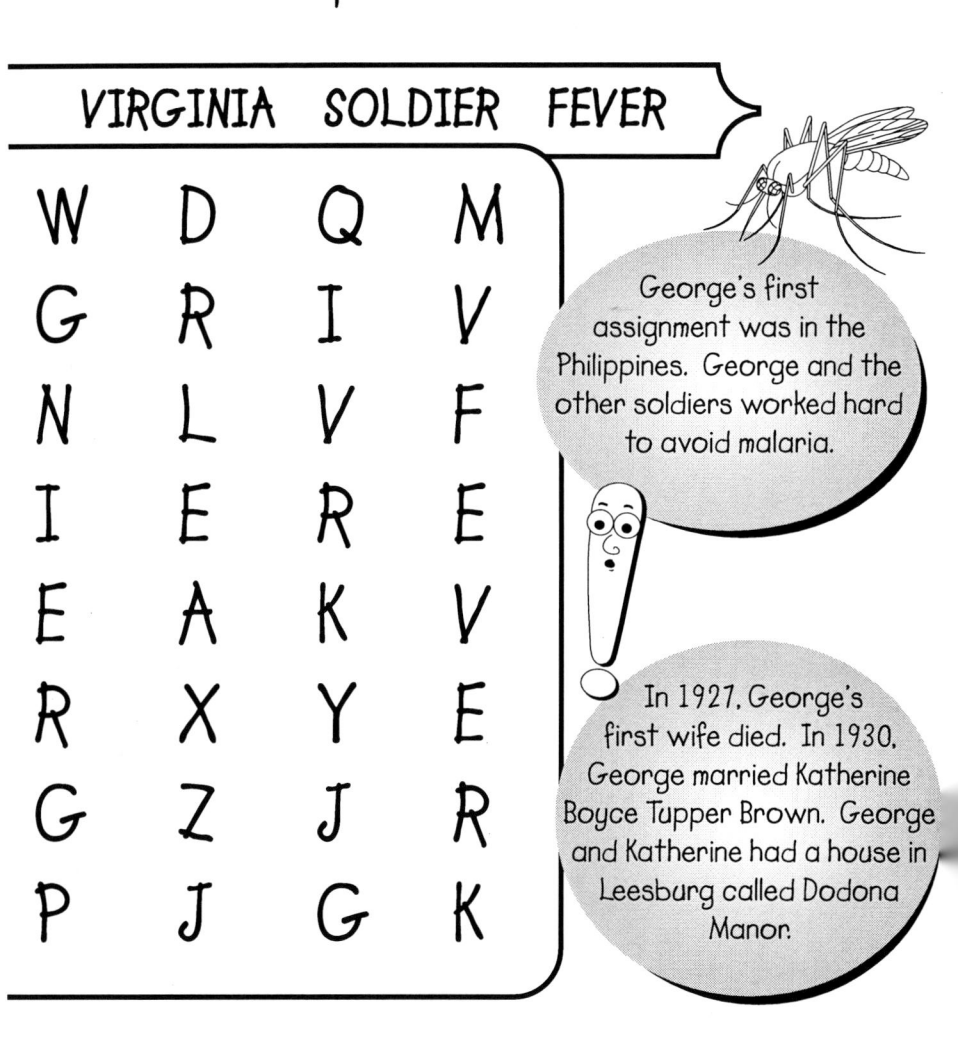

VIRGINIA SOLDIER FEVER

```
W  D  Q  M
G  R  I  V
N  L  V  F
I  E  R  E
E  A  K  V
R  X  Y  E
G  Z  J  R
P  J  G  K
```

George's first assignment was in the Philippines. George and the other soldiers worked hard to avoid malaria.

In 1927, George's first wife died. In 1930, George married Katherine Boyce Tupper Brown. George and Katherine had a house in Leesburg called Dodona Manor.

George had a long career in the United States Army. He served in the Philippines, France, and China. During World War I, he helped plan an attack on the Germans. He directed the movement of 400,000 men and 2,700 guns to the final American battle of the war. The Germans were completely surprised.

George supervised Civilian Conservation Corps camps during the Great Depression.

Number these events in the order they happened.

___ George was sick with typhoid fever.

___ George planned an attack on the Germans.

___ George attended school in Uniontown.

___ George married Elizabeth "Lily" Cole.

From 1927 to 1932, George was in charge of training at the Infantry School at Fort Benning, Georgia.

In 1939, George became the U.S. Army chief of staff with the rank of general. During World War II, he helped plan Operation Overlord or "D-Day." After the war, George came up with a "plan" to help a war-torn Europe recover.

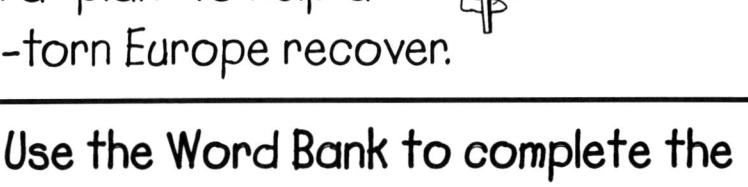

Use the Word Bank to complete the sentence.

George's plan was to _____ money to _____ in Europe over a _____-year period.

WORD BANK

four   give   countries

George was Secretary of State when he worked on the European Recovery Program.

In 1953, George was awarded the Nobel Peace Prize for the "European Recovery Program." He is most famous for this plan. George was the only professional soldier to ever win the Nobel Peace Prize. George C. Marshall died on October 16, 1959.

George's plan is also called the "Marshall Plan" after him.

Color the picture of General Marshall.

George was buried in Arlington National Cemetery.

Glossary

barracks: a building or group of buildings for soldiers to live in, usually in a fort or military camp

commission: a written order giving rank and authority as an officer in the armed forces.

malaria: a disease that causes chills and fever. Malaria is spread by mosquitoes.

Philippines: an island country in the southwest Pacific Ocean

typhoid: an infectious disease which is sometimes fatal. People can be inoculated against typhoid fever.

Pop Quiz!

1. Which school did George attend?
   - ○ The Virginia Military Institute
   - ○ United States Military Academy
   - ○ The Naval Academy

2. Which one was NOT related to George C. Marshall?
   - ○ Charles Marshall
   - ○ John Marshall
   - ○ Robert E. Lee

3. Who did George plan an attack against?
   - ○ Great Britain
   - ○ France
   - ○ Germany

4. What was the name of the plan to help Europe?
   - ○ European Recovery Program (Marshall Plan)
   - ○ European Discovery Program (Martial Law)
   - ○ European Rebuilding Program (Marshall Plan)

5. George's plan was to give money to Europe for what period of time?
   - ○ Forty days
   - ○ Four years
   - ○ Forty years